A New True Book

THE ICE AGE

By Darlene R. Stille

CHILDRENS PRESS®

CHICAGO

Pools of meltwater on a glacier
in Canada.

Library of Congress Cataloging-in-Publication Data

Stille, Darlene R.
    Ice age / by Darlene R. Stille.
        p.   cm. — (A New true book)
    Includes index.
    Summary: Describes the earth's many ice ages, with
an emphasis on the climate, people, and animals of the
last great ice age.
    IBSN 0-516-01107-3
    1. Glacial epoch—Juvenile literature.
2. Paleolithic period—Juvenile literature.
[1. Glacial epoch.] I. Title.
QE697.S816 1990   90-37681
551.7'92—dc20   CIP
                                        AC

TABLE OF CONTENTS

What Is an Ice Age? ...5

Earth's Many Ice Ages...7

The Last Ice Age...8

People of the Ice Age...11

How Ice Age People Lived...14

Animals of the Ice Age...18

How We Know About Ice Age
    Animals...23

How Did the Ice Age Mammals
    Die? ...28

The End of the Ice Age...33

The Next Ice Age...42

Words You Should Know...46

Index...47

A glacier in Norway flows down a valley like a river.

WHAT IS AN ICE AGE?

During an ice age the temperature is very cold over large parts of the earth. Great sheets of ice cover these places. The ice can be more than a mile thick.

The ice begins near the north and south poles. It flows out from there like a river. These rivers of ice are called glaciers.

Every year the glaciers get bigger. They grow because summer temperatures are

Mendenhall Glacier in Alaska

not warm enough to melt the
snow that falls during the
winter. As they grow, the
glaciers begin to flow. They
become very big and cover
huge areas. Then where the
glaciers are, there is winter
all year. There is always ice
and snow and cold.

EARTH'S MANY ICE AGES

There have been many ice ages since earth formed about 4.5 billion years ago. The first ice age started more than 2 billion years ago. Between the ice ages, there have been warm times when it was summer all over the earth all the time.

The ice ages lasted a long time. Some of them lasted for 50 million years! The last one, called the Ice Age, began 2 million years ago. It ended only about 10,000 years ago.

THE LAST ICE AGE

The last Ice Age is the one we know the most about. More than 2 million years ago, ice started to form in the Arctic Circle. There was also ice very far south in Antarctica.

In North America the Arctic ice came down as far south as Illinois and Missouri. Ice flowed out to cover Scandinavia and other parts of northern Europe.

A glacier carved out this U-shaped valley as it moved over the ground.

In some places there was no ice. In Africa and South America, the climate was warm. Farther north in the

9

The white areas on this map show the parts of the
world that glaciers covered during the last Ice Age.

southern parts of Europe
and North America, there
were seasons. Summers
were cooler, and winters
were very cold.

Plants and animals lived
in the warmer areas beyond
the ice sheets. People also
lived during the Ice Age.

Early Ice Age people made tools of chipped stone.

PEOPLE OF THE ICE AGE

Ice Age people are called prehistoric people because they lived in the time before written history. They are also called Stone Age people because they used tools made of stone.

Ice Age people lived south of the great ice sheets. Some lived in Europe. Some lived in Africa and Asia. Some lived in North America.

These people lived from 2 million years ago to about 8,000 years ago. During this time, the Ice Age people learned many things. But they never learned to write. So we cannot learn about them by reading stories they

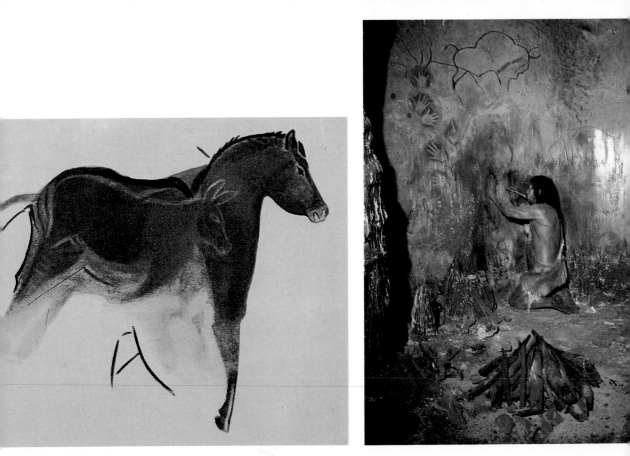

Ice Age people drew and painted pictures on the walls of caves (right). Most of the pictures were of animals, such as this horse and foal from Spain (left).

wrote. But they left behind
stone tools and paintings on
cave walls. These things tell
us something about them
and how they lived.

HOW ICE AGE PEOPLE LIVED

Some Ice Age people lived in caves. Most of them lived in tents made of animal skins. Later, they built simple huts.

Ice Age people learned to

Ice Age people hunted animals for meat. They lived in tents made of animal skins.

Stone axes (left) and spear points (right) made by
Ice Age people have been found in many places.

make simple stone tools.
They had stone axes and
stone knives. They had stone
points for spears and arrows.
They made their tools by
chipping one stone with
another. Later they learned
to make needles and other
tools out of bones.

15

Ice Age people used stone knives to cut up
their meat. They cooked it over open fires.

There were no farms
during the Ice Age. People
got meat by hunting. They
also gathered wild plants
and seeds for food. During
the Ice Age, people
discovered how to use fire
for cooking and for warmth.
Ice Age people who lived

Prehistoric people made fire by twirling a stick in a hole in wood until friction made the stick hot enough to make a flame.

close to the ice sheets in Europe and North America needed warm clothes. They made their clothes from animal skins. They made fur robes to keep warm in the cold winters. Some of them decorated their clothes with shells or quills.

ANIMALS OF THE ICE AGE

Animals of the Ice Age
were very different from
animals of today. During the
Ice Age there were many big
mammals. Mammals are

Some woolly mammoths were 14 feet tall. Their long
hair protected them from the cold of the Ice Age.

animals that feed their young with milk. These big Ice Age mammals no longer exist.

One of the biggest mammals was the woolly mammoth. It looked like a big shaggy elephant. The mastodon was a smaller beast that also looked like an elephant with big curving tusks.

19

Saber-toothed tigers on the hunt are watched by vultures.
The saber-toothed tiger's long fangs (inset) made it a great hunter.

One of the fiercest Ice
Age animals was the saber-
toothed tiger. It was a
prehistoric cat with two long
fangs. It used its fangs to kill
other animals for food.

20

One of the strangest Ice Age animals was the glyptodon. It looked like an armadillo. But it was as big as a lion!

Many Ice Age animals lived in caves. These animals included the cave bear and the cave lion. People who found skeletons of these big

Ice Age hunters attack a giant cave bear with their weapons of wood and stone.

Bones of mammoths (left) and saber-toothed tigers (right) have been found preserved in the earth.

mammals thousands of years later may have thought they were dragons.

Bigger versions of some animals alive today existed during the Ice Age. There were giant beavers as big as bears. There were giant deer with antlers the size of small trees.

HOW WE KNOW ABOUT ICE AGE ANIMALS

Scientists have found a few Ice Age mammoths frozen in the ice in Siberia.

This baby mammoth lived 10,000 years ago. It was found frozen in the ice in Siberia. The skin and hair can still be seen.

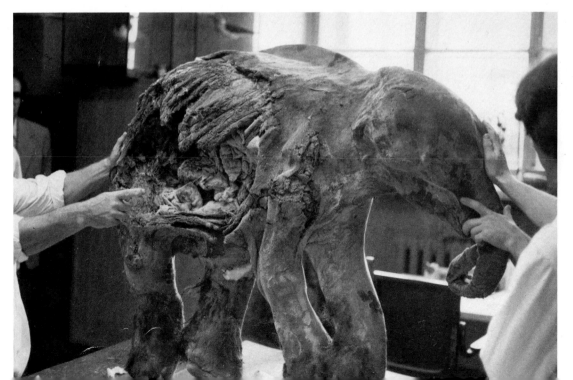

There are also many
bones of Ice Age animals
buried in many places. The
bones of more than a million
Ice Age animals have been
found in the La Brea tar pits
in Los Angeles. The animals
became trapped in the oily
tar when they came to drink
from the shallow pool of
water that covered it.

Opposite page: Even huge animals could not escape from the
La Brea tar pits. This model shows a mammoth trapped in the oily tar.

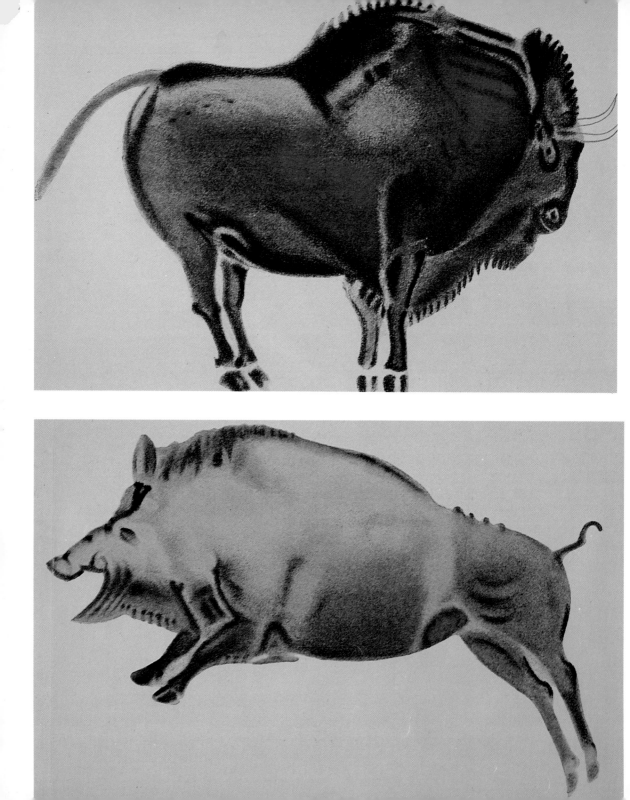

Ice Age people also left pictures of the animals. They made drawings on cave walls. They even made some statues. Because of these prehistoric artists, we know what some of the Ice Age animals looked like.

Opposite page: Ice Age paintings of a bull (top) and a boar (bottom) from a cave in Spain. The artists drew animals that they hunted.

HOW DID THE ICE AGE MAMMALS DIE?

The Ice Age mammals became extinct. This means they all died off. No one knows why this happened. But scientists have some theories.

A change to a warmer climate may have killed off the big mammals. As earth's temperature grew warmer, many things changed.

Scientists know what kinds of plants existed during the Ice Age because their remains have been preserved in rocks.

There were changes in the plants that the animals ate. Trees and grasses that grew well in the cold Ice Age climate died off. New plants took their place. Maybe the big mammals could not eat the new plants.

Maybe the big, thick-furred animals could not take the heat. They probably moved north as the ice melted. They may have run into other herds with strange diseases. The big mammals may have become sick and died.

Another theory says that prehistoric hunters may have killed off the animals. The Ice Age people may have killed many more animals than they needed.

Ice Age hunters surround a mammoth and bring it down with arrows.

Bands of hunters speared
woolly mammoths and other
animals one at a time. They
also killed whole herds at
once. The hunters would
surround the herd. They

would make noises to
frighten the animals and
then stampede the herd off a
steep cliff.

Any or all of these things
may have killed the big
mammals. But we may never
know for sure why they died
out.

THE END OF THE ICE AGE

One day the earth began
to grow warmer. As the
temperature warmed, the ice
began to melt. The glaciers
retreated. The moving ice
carved up the ground. It made
the world we know today.

Moving glaciers passed over these rocks and left them polished (left)
or covered with grooves and scratches (right).

Glaciers pushed past mountains and carved peaks into unusual shapes (left). Sometimes the glaciers made U-shaped valleys between the high rocks (right).

The glaciers dug out large and small holes in the ground. When the glaciers melted, some of these holes filled with water and became lakes. This is how the Great Lakes were made.

Glaciers carved these rock formations on the shores of Lake Superior.

The low hills formed by this glacial moraine
are covered with soil and plants.

As the ice melted, it left
behind piles and ridges of
rocks and gravel. These
ridges are called moraines.
There are hilly moraines
throughout the Midwest.

The moving ice also
ground up pebbles. This

made very fine soil. When the glaciers melted, this soil was carried by the wind to such places as the Great Plains.

The melting ice caused great floods. Much of the water went into the oceans. During the Ice Age, so much of earth's water was locked up in ice that the level of the oceans fell about 300 feet. Places that were above water during the Ice Age are now underwater.

A piece of land that once connected Alaska to Russia is under the sea. So is a land bridge that once connected England to Europe.

By 8,000 years ago, the glaciers had retreated north to where they are today. We can see glaciers in Canada and Alaska. Great ice sheets still cover Greenland and Antarctica. There are also

We can still see glaciers in Canada (above) and in Alaska (left). The tops of mountains can be seen above the huge ice sheet of Antarctica (below).

Cows graze in a summer meadow below frozen glaciers in the high Alps.

It is summer in Glacier National Park, but the ice sheet on the mountain never melts.

glaciers on high mountains
in Europe and Scandinavia.
We can see ice sheets in
Glacier National Park in
Montana.

THE NEXT ICE AGE

Some scientists think that another ice age will begin soon. They say that earth's temperature will start to drop.

Another ice age would not be unusual. Earth's climate is always changing. The way earth travels around the sun may make the temperature drop. Earth's orbit, or path, around the sun is not always the same. It changes over thousands of years.

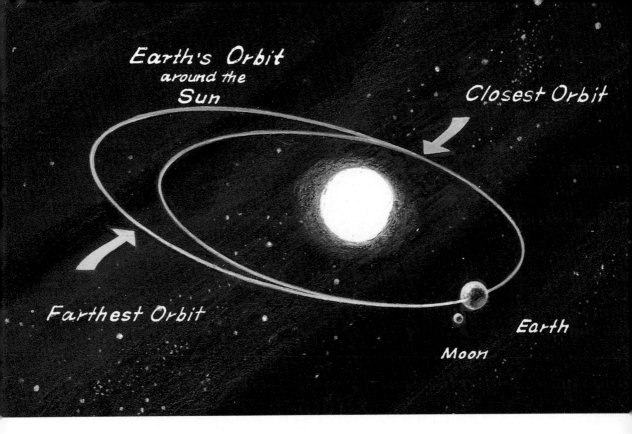

Earth's Orbit around the Sun

Closest Orbit

Farthest Orbit

Earth

Moon

Sometimes earth's orbit is closer to the sun. Sometimes it is farther away.

When it orbits close to the sun, earth is warmer. When its path takes earth far from the sun, earth is colder.

Earth also is tilted on its axis. Sometimes the tilt changes. This could also make earth cooler. Scientists think these kinds of changes in orbit and tilt might cause ice ages. But even if another ice age is on the way, we don't have to worry now. It will take many thousands of years for the ice sheets to form.

Opposite page: Fox Glacier in New Zealand

WORDS YOU SHOULD KNOW

Antarctica (ant • ARK • tih • ka) — a large landmass around the
South Pole, covered by ice sheets

antlers (ANT • lerz) — large branched horns that grow on the heads
of deer

Arctic Circle (ARK • tik   SIR • kil) — an imaginary line that goes
around the earth in the cold, far northern regions

armadillo (arm • ah • DIL • oh) — a burrowing animal that has bony
plates around its head and back

axis (AX • iss) — an imaginary straight line around which the earth
turns

cave (CAYVE) — an opening in the earth; a hollow place inside the
rocks of the earth

cliff (KLIHF) — a high steep rock face with little or no slope

climate (KLY • mit) — the average kind of weather at a specific
place

extinct (ek • STINKT) — no longer living

fangs (FANGZ) — long, sharp, front teeth

glacier (GLAY • sher) — a thick mass of snow and ice that moves
slowly across land or down a mountain

glyptodon (GLIP • ta • dahn) — a large prehistoric animal that was
covered with plates like an armadillo

mammal (MAM • il) — one of a group of warm-blooded animals that
have hair and nurse their young with milk

mammoth (MAM • uth) — a large, prehistoric animal that looked
like an elephant with long hair and curving tusks

mastodon (MASS • ta • dahn) — a large prehistoric animal that
looked like an elephant

moraines (mor • AYNZ) — hills and ridges made of gravel, rocks,
and sand pushed along and deposited by a glacier

orbit (OR • bit) — the path an object takes when it moves around
another object

prehistoric (pre • hiss • TOR • ik) — occurring before people invented writing

quill (KWILL) — the hollow base of a bird's feather

saber-toothed tiger (SAY • ber TOOTHT TY • ger) — a large prehistoric cat that had long fangs in the front of its mouth

Scandinavia (skan • duh • NAY • vee • ah) — a peninsula in the north of Europe

Siberia (sy • BEER • ee • ya) — huge area of land in northern Asia, part of the Soviet Union

skeleton (SKEHL • ih • tun) — the bones of an animal

stampede (stam • PEED) — a sudden, panicked rush of a herd of animals

theories (THEER • reez) — ideas about why or how something happens

INDEX

Africa, 9, 12
Alaska, 38
animals, 10, 17, 18-22, 23-27, 28-32
animal skins, 14, 17
Antarctica, 8, 38
antlers, 22
Arctic Circle, 8
Asia, 12
axis of earth, 45
beavers, 22
bones, 24
bone tools, 15

Canada, 38
cave art, 13, 27
cave bear, 21
cave lion, 21
caves, 13, 14, 21
climate, 9, 28, 29, 42
clothes, 17
deer, 22
diseases, 30
dragons, 22
earth, 5, 7, 42, 43, 45
England, 38
Europe, 8, 10, 12, 17, 38, 41

fangs, 20
fire, 16
floods, 37
Glacier National Park, 41
glaciers, 5, 6, 33, 34, 37, 38, 41
glyptodon, 21
gravel, 36
Great Lakes, 34
Great Plains, 37
Greenland, 38
hunting, 16, 30, 31-32
Illinois, 8
La Brea tar pits, 24
lakes, 34
land bridge, 38
length of ice ages, 7
Los Angeles, 24
mammals, 18, 22, 28, 29, 30
mastodon, 19
Midwest, 36
Missouri, 8
Montana, 41
moraines, 36

North America, 8, 10, 12, 17
oceans, 37
orbit of earth, 42-43
people, 10, 11-13, 14-17
plants, 10, 16, 29
poles, north and south, 5
quills, 17
rocks, 36
Russia, 38
saber-toothed tiger, 20
Scandinavia, 8, 41
seasons, 6, 10
shells, 17
Siberia, 23
snow, 6
soil, 37
South America, 9
statues, 27
Stone Age, 11
stone tools, 11, 13, 15
sun, 42, 43
temperature, 5, 10, 28, 33, 42
tusks, 19
woolly mammoth, 19, 23, 31

About the Author

Darlene R. Stille is a Chicago-based science writer and editor.